ELTON JOHN
THE BIG PICTURE

CW01584214

Exclusive Distributors

International Music Publications Limited
Southend Road, Woodford Green, Essex IG8 8HN, England

International Music Publications GmbH, Germany
Marstallstraße 8, D-80539 Munchen, Germany

Nuova Carish S.p.a.
Via Campania, 12 20098 S. Giuliano Milanese (MI)
Zona Industriale Sesto Ulteriano, Italy
25 Rue D'Hauteville, 75010 Paris, France

Danmusik
Vognmagergade 7, DK-1120 Copenhagen K, Denmark

Warner/Chappell Music Australia Pty Ltd.
3 Talavera Road, North Ryde, New South Wales 2113, Australia

Music Arranged by Jason Hazeley and Processed by Global Music Solutions, Surrey SM6 9BT
Printed by The Panda Group · Haverhill · Suffolk CB9 8PR · UK

ELTON JOHN

In 1974, Elton John was performing a charity concert for his beloved Watford Football Club at the team ground. The wife of an American record executive ran up and down the stairs of the Director's Box.......

"He's my generation's Sinatra!" she squealed. "He's my generation's Sinatra!"

The other guests were greatly amused. but nearly two dozen years late we have to admit that the woman was basically right. Of course, there are fundamental differences between Ol' Blue Eyes and Ol' Four Eyes. Fabulous Frank did not write his own material; Elton rarely sings songs of others. Sinatra was not an instrumentalist; EJ's piano playing is a fundamental part of his act.

But each man sustained a career of extraordinary duration in popular music, surviving setbacks to achieve new career goals and returning successfully from a period of rest. At the age of fifty, which he reached in 1997, Academy Award winning Elton is still at the centre of his profession, as Sinatra was in his fiftieth birthday year of 1965. For an Artist who has already sold in excess of 200 million records, the album releases are not as frantically paced as they were in earlier days, but each is still an event.

So it is with THE BIG PICTURE, the new Elton John album. Not only does it appear shortly after Elton reached his half century, and celebrated three decades in the music business, but it also comes out during the thirtieth anniversary of his songwriting partnership with lyricist Bernie Taupin.

Few collaborations in popular music thrive or even survive for this length of time. Indeed, Elton and Bernie have been writing together longer than the tenures of Lennon and McCartney, Bacharach and David, and Goffin and King combined. At the frantic peak of his American popularity in the mid-1970's Elton assembled a string of seven consecutive US number one albums in just three and a half years - a chart record pace only exceeded by The Beatles in the mid-60s. The albums in question were HONKY CHATEAU, DON'T SHOOT ME I'M ONLY THE PIANO PLAYER, GOODBYE YELLOW BRICK ROAD, CARIBOU, GREATEST HITS, CAPTAIN FANTASTIC AND THE BROWN DIRT COWBOY, and ROCK OF THE WESTIES. The GREATEST HITS album is one of the best-selling LP's in American history, with certified sales in the United States in excess of thirteen million. Elton even surpassed that total internationally with the soundtrack to the Disney film THE LION KING. The collection of songs he wrote with veteran stage and cinema lyricist Tim Rice was the number one album in the World for the year 1994. THE LION KING opened on Broadway in late 1997 with five new songs from the John-Rice duo, who have already completed their next Disney project, AIDA.

The occasional partnership with Tim Rice is an example of Elton's willingness to work with any individual whose talent he respects. EJ is the most sociable of all British chart Artists, succeeding with a record dozen different duet partners ranging from Aretha Franklin to RuPaul. The most recent joint success was "Live Like Horses", the John-Taupin song taken to the British top ten in late 1996 with Luciano Pavarotti. Elton's stirring solo version appears on THE BIG PICTURE.

Mr. John has also led the BILLBOARD Hot 100 with more chums than any other Artist. Of his eight number one singles, three are collaborations, each from a different decade. "Don't Go Breaking My Heart" with Kiki Dee was the Worlds number one single in 1976, "That's What Friends Are For" teamed Dionne Warwick with Elton, Gladys Knight and Stevie Wonder in 1985, and the live recording of "Don't Let The Sun Go Down On Me" by George Michael and Elton went to number one in both the US and UK in 1991.

EJ also featured prominently but without billing on mid-Seventies number ones by John Lennon ("Whatever Gets You Through The Night") and Neil Sedaka ("Bad Blood"). The former Beatle returned the favour by making a guest appearance on Elton's cover of his "Lucy In The Sky With Diamonds" under the name Dr. Winston O'Boogie. This was in the American charts on its way to number one, when Lennon made a famous guest appearance with Elton on Thanksgiving 1974 at Madison Square Garden. E. John has made John L. promise that if "Whatever Gets You Through The Night" got to number one in America, they would perform it in concert. Never thinking the song would be a big hit, Lennon agreed. He kept his end of the deal and, although terrified, came on stage to one of the most hysterical fan receptions in rock history. If roofs could be raised by sheer enthusiasm. the Garden would have blown its top that night.

Proceeds from both "That's What Friends Are For" and "Don't Let The Sun Go Down On Me" were dedicated to fighting AIDS, as have Elton's royalties on all his singles in the last several years. He began making this form of donation in Britain in 1990, just in time for his UK number one hit "Sacrifice", and started the same practice in America two years later, beginning with his international top ten hit "The One". Devastated at the loss of numerous friends and inspired by the courage of many others fighting the disease Elton resolved to use his energy and influence to make the contribution he could in the great struggle.

At the end of 1992 the star began one of the most successful charities in show business history, the Elton John AIDS Foundation. He wisely realised that to maximise its effectiveness in fund-raising, and to avoid exhausting himself to the point of diminishing returns, the Foundation had to raise money in ways other than the Artist's own performances.

An annual tennis tournament (with the more-than-a-mouthful title "Annual World Team Tennis All-Star 'Smash Hits' with Elton John and Billie Jean King") and a yearly Academy Awards Viewing party in Beverly Hills have been supported generously by the leading talents in sport and cinema, with each Individual event earning a six-figure sum for the Foundation. Other successful Initiatives included sales of the overflow from Elton's designer wardrobe, limited edition Oliver Peoples spectacles and restricted run Lalique crystal figurines. Film premieres and art auctions have also benefited the organisation. The Elton John AIDS Foundation has now disbursed millions of US dollars, UK pounds and Australian dollars to charities running effective programmes in their territories, as will as contributing to the fight against the disease in Africa, India and Thailand.

From Elton's now legendary US premiere at L.A.'s Troubadour nightclub in 1970, which led Robert Hilburn of The Los Angeles Times to predict the next day that "He's going to be one of rock's biggest and most important stars", he has become one of the most popular and successful recording Artists of all time. Along the way Elton found time to star as the Pinball Wizard in Ken Russell's film version of The Who's TOMMY, produce for Kiki Dee and Neil

Sedaka, form his own record label (Rocket), buy and sell Watford Football Club, work with Thom 'Philly Sound" Bell, break Madison Square Gardens box office records (twenty five sold out performances), as well as selling off a whole era of his own memorabilia and ephemera at the famous Sotheby's auction.

Elton John himself has reached that part of his life where generations of grateful fans around the world are simultaneously expressing their admiration with lifetime achievement awards. This is a polite way of stating the old Bette Davis maxim that if you hang around long enough, they make a legend out of you - in spite of the fact that Elton is entering one of the busiest and most musically diverse periods of his career. In the past four years alone, for example, Elton has been made a Commander of the British Empire, an Honorary Member of the Royal Academy of Music (the music school to which he won a scholarship aged 11), an Officer of Arts and Letters in France and a member of the Rock N' Roll Hall of Fame.These are all humbling awards whose spirit has been matched by other prizes from around the Globe recently, as well as the Polar Music Prize, a Grammy and a Brit. His favourite of his show business gongs are the Oscar and the Ivor Novello (the British songwriting award), if only because the trophies are the most attractive to put on the mantelpiece. Incidentally, to show the differences in national taste, it was "Can You Feel The Love Tonight" that was the Academy Award winner from THE LION KING but "Circle of Life" that nabbed the Ivor Novello.

Elton also holds distinctions for which there are no physical awards. When "Blessed" from his 1995 album MADE IN ENGLAND reached number one on the Adult Contemporary chart, it reinforced his standing as the all-time top Artist in the mass appeal format. He is one of the all-time top three stars of both the US and UK singles chart and is climbing the all-time top ten list of both countries' album Artists.

THE BIG PICTURE has only added to his success. The first track to hit the airwaves was the lead off single, "Something About The Way You Look Tonight." Following the tragic death of Diana, Princess of Wales, and the subsequent inclusion of Elton's version of "Candle in The Wind '97" in the funeral service, this single was released worldwide as a double A-side (Something About the Way You Look Tonight/Candle in the Wind '97"). This release went on to become the best selling single of all time - breaking records the world over.

A listener may feel that "Something About The Way You Look Tonight" would be at home on many country radio stations, and this would be apt. Elton himself professes that some of THE BIG PICTURE has undertones of TUMBLEWEED CONNECTION, the country-influenced album that did well for him and Bernie in 1971. Mr John is no stranger to the turntables and CD players of country stars, anyway. When Garth Brooks first appeared at the Wembley Arena, only a few miles from Elton's boyhood home, he informed his bemused audience that their local hero had been one of his idols, and performed a moving version of "Candle in the Wind" as a tribute.

That tune was both a hit in the UK both in its studio form in 1974 and in a live-in-Australia reading in 1988. Bernie Taupin claimed to get the title image for the Marilyn Monroe tribute from record executive Clive Davis, who told him his deceased star Janis Joplin had been a "candle in the wind". When the reporter quoting Taupin asked Davis if he recalled the remark, he replied he could not remember saying it. So it is that songs take on lives and meanings of their own. At one point Elton thought he knew whom 'Your Song" was about, but Bernie denied it, and never revealed who inspired what has become a pop classic. Because Elton chose not to include Bernie's last verse in the recording of "Daniel", some listeners thought the song about a one-eyed war veteran trying to find peace in Spain was a gay love ballad.

If there are any arguments that need to be settled, let it be said that the 1975 US number one "Philadelphia Freedom" was indeed inspired by Billie Jean King's tennis team, the Philadelphia Freedoms. "Tiny Dance" was written about Bernie's Californian girlfriend Maxine. The life saver in "Someone Saved My Life Tonight" was Long John Baldry, who convinced Elton to cancel his first engagement to be married. Stevie Wonder played harmonica on "I Guess That's Why They Call It The Blues," Dusty Springfield sang backing vocal on "The Bitch Is Back", and George Michael helped out on "Nikita".

For all the guest stars who appear on Elton John albums, and this time they include Paul Carrack (organ on "Something About The Way You Look Tonight") and the Last London Gospel Choir (vocals on "The River Can Bend"), the Artist is aware that he owes a great deal of his success to his team of associates. He has only ever had two long-term producers, Gus Dudgeon and Chris Thomas, and it is the latter who on THE BIG PICTURE is once again at the helm. Not only has Elton written with Bernie Taupin for thirty years, he has been managed by John Reid for more than a quarter of a century. In addition, guitarist Davey Johnstone, who originally joined the Elton John band in 1972, is part of the group this time too.

It is always difficult to foretell what track will emerge as the most memorable from an album. In the United States, for example, "Border Song" was the first single from the ELTON JOHN album not "Your Song". "Bennie and the Jets" was only released from GOODBYE YELLOW BRICK ROAD when a promotion man promised it would be a Rhythm and Blues hit. (It was, which thrilled R&B lover Elton.) "I Guess That's Why They Call It The Blues" was the third choice from the 1983 set TOO LOW FOR ZERO, released only after it had been a top five British success.

THE BIG PICTURE offers a powerful selection of words and music - love and loss, healing and hope - life's essential matters coupled with some of the strongest music of Elton's career. "Live Like Horses" is a classic Elton John ballad, building to a powerful climax that leaves the listener exhausted, strong enough only to push the play button again. "Recover Your Soul" is a grower, but might be held back by the fact that the song itself seems to want to be called "Release" instead, but then again, Elton Is an Artist who actually scored an American top forty hit with a single called "I Feel Like A Bullet (In The Gun of Robert Ford)", - suggesting he and thirty-year partner Bernie can call their songs what they want.

"If the River Can Bend" features rousing gospel call-and-response vocals, and "Love's Got a Lot to Answer For" in with its indelible bass line and luminous lyric ("Freedoms like the stars in the sky/Alone and cold and burning"). In the end, some listeners will prefer the emotional lyrics of the title track "The Big Picture", in which Elton's elegant keyboard intercuts with acoustic guitar. "On and on," Taupin writes and Elton sings, "the story of our lives goes on and on." It is a long story, and a very big picture.

John Reid Enterprises

November 1997

LONG WAY FROM HAPPINESS

I guess you're okay / You seem to feel better these days / I've known you for so long / I've seen your brightness go from blue to grey

You know that's true / You can shake your head but I can prove / I've seen things through your eyes / You think you win but in the end you lose

There's no second guess / We take no second bets / Chances are / We're a long way from happiness / Don't cover up the road to love / With words that can't express / The truth implies / You're high and dry / A long way from happiness

I'm one step behind / Looking out for you all the time / I'll put my faith in you / And steer you clear of love that leaves you blind

There's no second guess / We take no second bets / Chances are / We're a long way from happiness / Don't cover up the road to love / With words that can't express / The truth implies / You're high and dry / A long way from happiness ⊙

"There's no second guess, we take no second bets

...chances are we're a long way from happiness

LIVE LIKE HORSES

I can't control this flesh and blood / That's wrapped around my bones / It moves beneath me like a river / Into the great unknown / I stepped onto the moving stairs / Before I could tie my shoes / Pried a harp out of the fingers of a renegade / Who lived and died the blues

And his promise made was never clear / It just carved itself in me / All I saw was frost inside my hand / On the night he said to me

Someday / We'll live like horses / Free rein / From your old iron fences / There's more ways than one / To regain your senses / Break out the stalls / And we'll live like horses

We're the victims of the heartbreak / That kept us short of breath / Trapped above these bloodless streets / Without a safety net / I stood in line to join the tribe / One more customer of fate / Claimed a spoke in the wheel of the wagon train / On the road to the golden gate

On the flat dry desert I jumped ship / It just made sense to me / I've spent too long in the belly of the beast / And now I shall be free / Someday / We'll live like horses / Free rein / From your old iron fences There's more ways than one / To regain your senses / Break out the stalls / And we'll live like horses ⊙

LOVE'S GOT A LOT TO ANSWER FOR

Pull my coat around me / Feel the cold wind haunt me / Streets are empty just like me / The murmour of an echo / Seems to come from every window / is loneliness the same as being free

I guess I must have been dreaming / To think that I believed in you at all / Now I just can't fight it / As the shadow of the night begins to fall

Love's got a lot to answer for / Oh I just can't sleep with this feeling anymore / Let the cold night air cool the heat / Of two hearts gone to war / For no matter who wins, in the end / Love's got a lot to answer for

All I need is darkness / The best of all protection / Freedom's like the stars in the sky / Alone and cold and burning / Each one keeps it's distance / if only we were stars you and I

Oh I guess I must have been dreaming / To think that I believed in you at all / And now I just can't fight it / As the shadow of the night begins to fall

Love's got a lot to answer for / Oh I just can't sleep with this feeling anymore / Let the cold night air cool the heat / Of two hearts gone to war / For no matter who wins, in the end / Love's got a lot to answer for

Love's got a lot to answer for / Oh I just can't sleep with this feeling anymore / Let the cold night air cool the heat / Of two hearts gone to war / For no matter who wins, in the end / Love's got a lot to answer for

No matter who wins, in the endLove's got a lot to answer for ⊙

THE END WILL COME

And when we start we say forever / We say we care, we need, we feel / We read the movement of our eyes / But in our hearts we still believe

The end will come, before we know / The silent rule of love applies / We light the fuse and let it burn out / We just accept that love must die

And so they say, the end will come for us / And so the world, slows down to let us off / Just hang it up and let it go, accept it if I must / But I don't believe, I don't believe that the end will come for us / No I won't believe the end will come for us

The end will come like sudden rain / The end is never what it seems / We sink the ship before we sail / We just accept what failure means

And so they say, the end will come for us

/ And so the world, slows down to let us off / Just hang it up and let it go, accept it if I must / But I don't believe, I don't believe that the end will come for us / No I won't believe the end will come for us ⊙

"We read the movement of our eyes but in our hearts we still believe"

IF THE RIVER CAN BEND

I don't know what to say / I don't know where the light shines / it's a grey dawn rising on a green hill / And there's so much behind us

Come and embrace the struggle / But win or lose we live here / Build a new beginning on an old rock / Breathe deep of the sweet fresh air

With your harmony if the river can bend, Yeah / I'll find you waiting / Home at last from the wild sea / All the twists and turns / We've made together / All the boats you rocked /

I don't know where we go / I sure feel there's something out there / There's a great awakening and a new morning / And your spirits pounding loud and clear

if the river can bend / I'll find you waiting / Home at last from the wild sea / All the twists and turns

We've made together / All the boats you rocked / With your harmony / if the river can bend / if the river can bend / if the river can bend / if the river can bend

if the river can bend / I'll find you waiting / Home at last from the wild sea / All the twists and turns / We've made together / All

"Your spirits pounding loud and clear"

the boats you rocked / With your harmony / if the river can bend

if the river can bend / I'll find you waiting / Home at last from the wild sea / All the twists and turns / We've made together / All the boats you rocked /

With your harmony / if the river can bend / Yeah / if the river can bend / Yeah,Yeah

if the river can bend /
if the river can bend /
if the river can bend /
if the river can bend

Yeah / if the river can bend / Yeah
Yeah / if the river can bend / Yeah

if the river can bend / (repeat) ⊙

RECOVER YOUR SOUL

"RELEASE, RELAX, LET GO"

Baby your missing / Something in the air / I gotta name but it don't matter / What's going on / it's cold in here /

You have a life but it's torn and tattered

Maybe you're losing / Pieces of your heart / You have a world but it stopped turning / You lose the day / And gain the dark / Love was a fire but it stopped burning

So spare your heart save your soul / Don't drag your love across the coals / Find your feet and your fortune can be told / Release, relax, let go / And hey now let's recover / And hey now let's recover / Hey now let's recover your soul

Lazy old sunset / Sinking like a tear / Alone at night in a losing battle / That perfect world / is never clear / You have to fight for the things that matter

So spare your heart save your soul / Don't drag your love across the coals / Find your feet and your fortune can be told / Release, relax, let go / And hey now let's recover / And hey now let's recover / Hey now let's recover your soul

So spare your heart save your soul / Don't drag your love across the coals / Find your feet and your fortune can be told / Release, relax, let go / And hey now let's recover / Hey now let's recover / Hey now let's recover your soul / Hey now let's recover your soul ⊙

I CAN'T STEER MY HEART CLEAR OF YOU

Take me for granted, I think that I could stand it / After all these rough seas / Left me reckless and abandoned / Say the spirits willing, chance a new beginning / Break down the cold front / Give me peace and understanding

And you wait, and you wonder / Will she still beat the drum and bring the thunder / Will she still be the star to see me through / 'Cause I can't steer my heart clear of you

No I can't steer my heart clear of you / it's the way it's been, ever since you sailed / Out of a storm and into view / And should I drift away, the compass holds the clue / You control the weather / And I can't steer my heart clear of you

Make me your penance, show me your innocence / Everything is history / From the aching to the pleasure / We enjoy the torture, the slow pain that it taught us / Everything gets twisted / Let me burn or bring me water

And you wait, and you wonder / Will she still beat the drum and bring the thunder / Will she still be the star to see me through / 'Cause I can't steer my heart clear of you

No I can't steer my heart clear of you / it's the way it's been, ever since you sailed / Out of a storm and into view / And should I drift away, the compass holds the clue / You control the weather / And I can't steer my heart clear of you

You control the weather / And I can't steer my heart clear of you ⊙

WICKED DREAMS

It's written clear across the room / in silent words the blind could understand / I came here to relax and

"Behind my eyes I'll wait for you"

find / A sleep that soaks me up like surf and sand

And as you appear as I descend / A soft outline all poised and feather light / I come into the darkness now / To conjure up a dream and close my eyes

Don't disturb me if you dare / Join me if you have the nerve / I'll show you where the best of me has been / Behind my eyes I'll wait for you / imagine just what we could do /

Come join me in my wicked dream

Don't send me back to real life / The daily grind just leaves me feeling numb / Leave me in my wicked dream / Where pressure cracks and beauty comes undone

Don't disturb me if you dare / Join me if you have the nerve / I'll show you where the best of me has been / Behind my eyes I'll wait for you / imagine just what we could do / Come join me in my wicked dream

Don't disturb me if you dare / Join me if you have the nerve / I'll show you where the best of me has been / Behind my eyes I'll wait for you / imagine just what we could do / Come join me in my wicked...

Come join me in my wicked...

Come join me in my wicked dream ⊙

THE BIG PICTURE

> "Wanna be your main man in..."

On and on / The story of our lives goes on and on / The path of time / The sunsets up ahead roll along

in your eyes / The option of a warm embrace implies / You're my friend / Happy endings keep our love alive

And tell me do I fit in the big picture / Do I have a shot at the big part / 'Cause I've been up all night looking at the big picture / I've got some good lines for my big star

Wanna be your main man in the big picture / What a deal / To get a part like this

Day to day / The shifting wind just blows us on our way / Here and there / Our pockets full of things to say Oh my love / I proudly represent you in this world / Little satellite

Brightest star tonight, oh my love / And tell me do I fit in the big picture / Do I have a shot at the big part / 'Cause I've been up all night looking at the big picture / I've got some good lines for my big star

Hope I got a future in the big picture / At the last embrace / From the first kiss

And tell me do I fit in the big picture / Do I have a shot at the big part / 'Cause I've been up all night looking at the big picture / I've got some good lines for my big star ⊙

JANUARY

Must have been the right month / Must have been a good time / Must have counted every cloud in the sky that night / Every single glass of wine

Must have learned some home truths / Sitting in that cool grass / Must have counted every blade in that emerald field / Every shooting star that passed

Should of had a talk with God / Sitting in the great unknown / Watching all the lovers in the world get together / Sitting in Heaven all alone

And we were love's knot after summer / Tied together in the dead of winter / Wrapped up with spring fever in the air / Bound together in the autumn / Every month means a little something / But January is the month that cares

Must have kissed you 'till I hurt you / Must have been a wild night / Must have rolled in the ashes at the break of day / Rag dolls in the morning light

Must have found a secret place / Hiding in our own world / Must have counted every smile on your sweet lips / Every single sound we heard

Should have had a talk with God / Sitting in the great unknown / Watching all the lovers in the world get together / Sitting in Heaven all alone

And we were love's knot after summer / Tied together in the dead of winter / Wrapped up with spring fever in the air / Bound together in the autumn / Every month means a little something / But January is the month that cares / January is the month that cares ⊙

SOMETHING ABOUT THE WAY YOU LOOK TONIGHT

> "it's that feeling I get about you, deep inside"

There was a time / I was everything and nothing all in one / When you found me / I was feeling like a cloud across the sun / I need to tell you / How you light up every second of the day / But in the moonlight / You just shine like a beacon on the bay

And I can't explain / But it's something about the way you look tonight / Takes my breath away / it's that feeling I get about you, deep inside / And I can't describe / But it's something about the way you look tonight / Takes my breath away / The way you look tonight

With your smile / You pull the deepest secrets from my heart / in all honesty / I'm speechless and I don't know where to start

And I can't explain / But it's something about the way / you look tonight / Takes my breath away / it's that feeling I get about you, deep inside / And I can't describe / But it's something about the way you look tonight / Takes my breath away / The way you look tonight

And I can't explain / But it's something about the way you look tonight / Takes my breath away / it's that feeling I get about you, deep inside / And I can't describe / But it's something about the way you look tonight / Takes my breath away / The way you look tonight ⊙

Long Way From Happiness

Words and Music by
Elton John and Bernie Taupin

2.3.
B♭
F
And there's no sec-ond guess we take no sec-ond bets, chan-ces
C
F
B♭
are we're a long way from hap-pi-ness. Don't cov-er up the road to love with words that
F
C
C♯dim7
Dm
can't ex-press, the truth im-plies you're high and dry and you're a
B♭add9
Cadd9
B♭add9/D
Cadd9/E
long way from hap-pi-ness.

B♭add9
Cadd9
Dm
B♭
Am7
to Coda
Dm
D.𝄋 al Coda
CODA
B♭
And there's no sec - ond guess, we take no
F
C
F
sec - ond bets, chan - ces are we're a long way from hap - pi - ness don't cov - er

B♭ F C C♯dim7
up the road to love with words that can't ex - press the truth im - plies you're high and dry,
Dm B♭add9 Cadd9 B♭add9
and you're a long way from hap - py a long way from
Cadd9 B♭add9/D Cadd9/E Fsus4
hap - py a long way from hap - pi - ness.

Cadd9/E
B♭add9
Cadd9
B♭add9/D
Cadd9/E
Fsus4
Cadd9/E
B♭add9
Cadd9
Dm
B♭
Am7
B♭add9
Cadd9
B♭add9
Cadd9
E♭6sus2

Live Like Horses

Words and Music by
Elton John and Bernie Taupin

B♭m E♭m A♭sus4 A♭
riv-er in-to the great un-known.
streets with-out a safe - ty net.
A♭/D♭ G♭6/D♭
I stepped on - to the mov-ing stairs
I stood in line to join the tribe,
A♭/D♭ G♭6/D♭
be-fore I could tie my shoes. Pried a harp out the fin-gers of a
one more cus-to-mer of fate. Claimed a spoke in the wheel of the
B♭m E♭m
re-ne-gade who lived and died the blues,
wa-gon train on the road to the Gold-en

A♭7sus4
A♭
B♭m
and his pro-mise made was ne - ver clear.
gate, on the flat dry des - ert, and jumped ship.
G♭
A♭sus4
It just carved it - self in me.
It just made sense to me.
A♭
A♭sus4
A♭
B♭m
All I saw was frost in - side my hand on the
I'll spend too long in the bel - ly of the beast and now
G♭
A♭sus4
night he said to me.
I shall be free.

A♭
D♭
A♭/C
Some - day we'll live like hors - es free rein
B♭m
A♭/C
G♭
from your old iron fen - ces there's more ways than one to re - gain your sen -
D♭/A♭
G♭/B♭
A♭7/C
1.
D♭
- ses, break out the stalls and we'll live like hors- es.
A♭/C
B♭m
G♭6
A♭

2.
D♭
A♭/C
B♭m
A♭/C
horses some day, free rein from your old iron fences there's more ways than
G♭
D♭/A♭
G♭/B♭
one to regain your senses break out the stalls and we'll live
A♭7/C
D♭
B♭m/D♭
G♭/D♭
D♭
like horses.

The End Will Come

Words and Music by
Elton John and Bernie Taupin

Am
C
Am
1. The end will come_ be-fore we know,___ the si - lent rule_ of love ap -
2. The end will come_ like sud-den rain,___ the end is ne - ver what it
3. (Instrumental)
C
B♭
Dm
-plies. We light the fuse_ and let it burn out,
seems. We sink the ship_ be - fore we sail,
Gm7
C
F
E♭
we just ac - cept_ that love must die.___
we just ac - cept_ what fail - ure means.___ And so they say the end will
C
F
A♭
B♭add9
come for us_ and so the world slows down to let us off.___ Just hang it up_

F
Gm7
F/A
B♭
— and let it go, — ac - cept it if — I must but I don't be - lieve,
F/C
B♭/D
1.2.
E♭/G
B♭/F
F
E♭
B♭/D
— I don't be - lieve that the end will come — for us — no I don't be - lieve the end will
A♭
C7
F
3.
E♭/G
B♭/F
come for — us.
End will come for us — just hang it up —
F
Gm7
F/A
B♭
— and let it go, — ac - cept it if — I must — but I don't be - lieve, —

F/C
B♭/D
E♭/G
B♭/F
F
E♭
B♭/D
I don't be lieve that the end will come for us no I don't be - lieve the end will
A♭
C7
F
come for us.
E♭
B♭/D
A♭
C7
F
E♭
B♭/D
A♭
C7
F
E♭
B♭/D
A♭
C7
F

If The River Can Bend

Words and Music by
Elton John and Bernie Taupin

G C/G G D/G Em Em7 Em Em7
I don't know where we go. I sure feel there's some-thing out there. There's a
Come and em - brace the strug-gle, but, win or lose, we live here. Build a
C Em D
great a-waken - ing and a new morn - ing and your spi - rit's pound-ing loud and clear.
new be-gin - ning on an old rock, breathe the deep of the sweet fresh air.
Dsus4 D F C G
If the riv - er can bend, I'll find you wait - ing, home at last from the
Dm F Am C
wild sea. All the twists and turns we've made to-ge-ther, all the boats you rocked with your

1.2.
G D Cm/E♭ A♭6 B♭/D Gm
har - mo - ny. If the ri-ver can bend. If the ri-ver can bend. If the
Cm A♭6 D7
ri-ver can bend. If the ri-ver can bend.
3.
D
har - mo-ny. If the
F C G Dm
ri-ver can bend, I'll find you wait - ing. Home at last from the wild sea.
F Am C
All the twists and turns we've made to-ge-ther, all the boats you've rocked with your

G D Cm/E♭ A♭6 B♭/D Gm
fr 4
fr 3
har - mo - ny. If the ri-ver can bend. If the ri-ver can bend. If the
Cm A♭6 D7 G B♭6
ri-ver can bend. If the ri - ver can bend. Yeah!
C G B♭6 C
If the ri-ver can bend.__ Yeah! Yeah! If the
Cm/E♭ A♭6 B♭/D Gm Cm A♭6
ri-ver can bend. If the ri-ver can bend. If the ri-ver can bend. If the

D7
G
B♭6
C
ri-ver can bend. Yeah! Yeah! If the ri-ver can bend.
G
B♭6
C
G
B♭6
C
— Yeah! Yeah! Yeah! If the ri-ver can bend.
G
B♭6
C
Cm/E♭
A♭6
fr 4
— Yeah! Yeah! If the ri-ver can bend. If the
B♭/D
Gm
fr 3
Cm/E♭
A♭6
fr 4
B♭/D
Gm
fr 3
repeat and fade
ri-ver can bend. If the ri-ver can bend. If the ri-ver can bend. If the

Love's Got A Lot To Answer For

Words and Music by
Elton John and Bernie Taupin

C D Bm Em
lone - li - ness the same as be - ing free?
on - ly we were stars you and I.
And I guess I must have been dream - ing to think that
C Am Bm Em C Am D
I be - lieved in you at all. Now I just can't fight it as the sha - dow of the night be - gins to fall.
E♭ A♭ B♭ E♭ A♭
fr 6 fr 4 fr 6 fr 6 fr 4
Love's got a lot to ans - wer for. Oh, I just can't sleep with this
B♭ E♭ A♭ B♭ G/B Cm
fr 6 fr 6 fr 4 fr 3
feel - ing a - ny more. Let the cold night air cool the heat of

E♭/G
A♭
B♭
Cm
D
Gm
two hearts gone to war.
For no mat-ter who wins in the end,
Am7♭5
A♭
E♭/G
1.
E♭/B♭
B♭7
E♭
Love's got a lot to ans - wer for.
2.
E♭/B♭
B♭7
E♭
Bm
Em
C
Am
ans - wer for.

Bm Em C D Bm Em C Am
Bm Em C Am7 D
E♭ A♭ B♭ E♭ A♭
Love's got a lot to ans - wer for. Oh I just can't sleep with this
B♭ E♭ A♭ B♭ G/B Cm
feel - ing a - ny - more. Let the cold night air cool the heat of

E♭/G
A♭
B♭
Cm
D
two hearts gone to war.
For no mat-ter who wins
Gm
Am7♭5
A♭
E♭/G
in the end
love's got a lot to
E♭/B♭
B♭7
E♭
Cm
D
Gm
Am7♭5
ans - wer for.
No mat-ter who wins
in the end
rit.
A♭
E♭/G
E♭/B♭
B♭7
E♭
love's got a lot to ans - wer for.

Something About The Way You Look Tonight

Words and Music by
Elton John and Bernie Taupin

F♯
A♯m7
Oh I need to tell you how you light up ev - ery sec - ond of the day,
smile you pull the deep - est sec - rets from my heart.
D♯m
F♯/C♯
B
but in the moon - light you just
In all hon - est - y I'm
G♯m7
C♯
shine like a bea - con on the bay.
speech - less and I don't know where to start.
And I can't ex -
F♯
A♯7
D♯m
- plain but it's some - thing a - bout the way you look to - night.

D♯7
G♯m
G♯m7
It takes my breath a - way.
It's that feel - ing I get a - bout you
C♯
F♯
deep in - side.
And I can't des - cribe
but it's
A♯7
D♯m
F♯/C♯
B
F♯/A♯
fr 3
G♯m
F♯
some - thing a - bout the way you look to - night.
It takes my breath a - way,
C♯
the way you look to - night.
1.
F♯
C♯
With your

2.
F♯
A
B
F♯
fr 4
night.
The way you look to - night. The way you
look to - night. The way you look to - night. The way you
look to - night. The way you look to - night. The way you look to - night.
The way you look to - night. The way you look to - night.

The Big Picture

Words and Music by
Elton John and Bernie Taupin

E♭ A♭ Gm7/D Gm7 Cm G7
In your eyes, the op - tion of a warm em - brace im - plies, you're my friend,
Oh, my love I proud - ly rep - re - sent you in this world lit - tle sa - tel - lite,
Cm G7 Cm F7/A B♭ B♭7
— hap - py end - ings keep our love a - live. And
— bright - est star to - night oh, my love.
E♭ D♭ A♭ E♭ F G♭
tell me do I fit in the big pic - ture? Do I have a shot at the
A♭ B♭ E♭ D♭ A♭ E♭
big part? 'Cause I've been up all night look - ing at the big pic - ture,

F F/A B♭ Cm A♭ B♭ Gm
I've got some good lines for my big star.
Wan-na be your main man in the big pic-ture.
Hope I got a fu-ture in the big pic-ture.
1.
A♭ Fm6 G/D G
What a deal to get a part like this.
2.
A♭ D7/F♯ G B♭7
at the last em-brace from the first kiss. And

E♭ D♭ A♭ E♭ F G♭
tell me do I fit in the big picture? do I have a shot at the
A♭ B♭ E♭ D♭ A♭ E♭
big part? 'Cause I've been up all night looking at the big picture,
F G♭ A♭ A♭6 E♭ D♭
I've got some good lines for my big star.
A♭ E♭ D♭/E♭ A♭/E♭ E♭
allarg.

Recover Your Soul

Words and Music by
Elton John and Bernie Taupin

C
B7
Em
What's go - ing on? It's cold in here,
C
G/B
D
you have a life but it's torn and tat - tered.
G
D/F♯
Em
G/D
May - be you're los - ing piec - es of your heart.
La - zy old sun - set sink - ing like a tear.
C
G/B
D
G/D
D
Dsus4
D
You have a world but it stopped turn - ing.
A - lone at night in a los - ing bat - tle.

C
B7
Em
Em7
You lose the day and gain the dark.
That per-fect world is ne - ver clear.
C
G/B
D
Love was a fire but it stopped burn - ing.
You have to fight for the things that mat - ter.
Spare your heart,
C
G
Am
Em
save your soul don't drag your love a-cross the coals.
Find your feet,
C
G
D
G/D
D
and your for - tune can be told.
Re-lease,

Am B7 Em G/D C
relax, let go and
D G G7/D C/G D G
hey now let's re - cov - er your soul.
D/G Em Em7 C
G/B Am7
1. 2.
Spare your heart,

C G Am Em
save your soul don't drag your love a-cross the coals. Find your feet
C G D G/D D
and your for-tune can be told. Re-lease,
Am B7 Em G/D C
re-lax, let go and
D G G7/D C/G D G G7/D C/G
hey now let's re-cov-er, hey now let's re-cov-er, hey

D G G7/D C/G D G D/F♯
now let's re - cov - er your soul.
Em C D G G7/D C/G D
and hey now let's re - cov - er your
G D/G Em Em7
soul.
C G/B Am7 rit. Gadd9

January

Words and Music by
Elton John and Bernie Taupin

E♭ F G C/G
-gle glass of wine. Must have learned some home truths,
the morn-ing light. Must have found a se-cret place,
E♭ F C Csus4 C
sit-ting in that cool grass, must have count-ed ev-ery
hid-ing in our own world, must have count-ed ev-ery
G E♭ F
blade in that emer-ald field, ev-ery shoot-ing star that passed.
smile on your sweet, sweet lips, ev-ery sin-gle sound we heard.

C F E♭ F11 C
Should have had a talk with God, sit - ting
F E♭ F11 C F/A A♭
in the great un - known, watch - ing all the lov - ers in the world
C/G Dm7 G7
get to - ge - ther sit - ting in hea - ven all a - lone. And we were
Cm7 C11 F C/E
love's knot af - ter sum - mer tied to - ge - ther in the dead of win - ter

E♭
F
C
wrapped up with spring fev - er in the air.
Cm7
C11
F
Bound to - ge - ther in the au - tumn ev - ery month means a lit -
C/E
D
A♭
B♭
- tle some - thing but Jan - u - a - ry is the month that cares.
1.
C
G
E♭maj7
Fadd9
Gadd9
E♭maj7
Fadd9

2.
C Csus4 C D A♭7 B♭
Jan - u - a - ry is the month that cares.
C G E♭maj7 Fadd9 Gadd9 E♭maj7 Fadd9
D A♭ B♭ C G E♭maj7
Fadd9 Gadd9 E♭maj7 Fadd9
repeat and fade

I Can't Steer My Heart Clear Of You

Words and Music by
Elton John and Bernie Taupin

G♭
B♭m
Say the spi - rit's will - ing, chance a new be - gin - ning,
We en - joy the tor - ture, the slow pain that it taught us,
C♭
A
break down the cold front, give me peace and un - der - stand - ing.
ev - ry - thing gets twist - ed let me burn or bring me wa - ter. And you
C♯m
G♯m/D♯
A
E
wait and you won - der, will she still beat the drum and bring the thun - der. Will she
B
C♯m
A
A/G
F6
still be the star to see me through? 'Cause I can't steer my heart clear of you.

G
E
G7
No I can't steer my heart clear of you,_ it's the
C
Am
Am7
way it's been_ ev - er since you sailed_ out of a storm_ and
B7
Em
Em/D
fr 3
in - to view. And should I drift a - way, the com - pass holds the
C
A♭
fr 4
clue. You con - trol the wea - ther and I

B♭9add4
1.
Csus4
A♭
can't steer my heart clear of you.
E♭m7
A♭
E♭m7
2.
Csus4
C
you.
You con-trol the
A♭
B♭9add4
Csus4
wea- ther,
and I can't steer my heart clear of you.

Wicked Dreams

Words and Music by
Elton John and Bernie Taupin

F Am G
surf and sand.
C F G
And you appear as I descend,
Don't send me back to real life,
(3rd time instrumental)
Am F G
a soft outline all poised and feather-light.
the daily grind just leaves me feeling numb.
Am F G Em
I come into the darkness now to conjure up a dream and
Leave me in my wicked dream where pressure cracks and beauty

F D7/F♯ G7
close my eyes.
comes un - done.
Am F G Am F G
(1.2.3.) Don't dis-turb me if you dare, join me if you have the nerve, I'll
C Am F G
show you where the best of me has been. Be -
Am F G Am F
-hind my eyes I'll wait for you. I - mag - ine just what we

Printed in England
The Panda Group · Haverhill · Suffolk · 2/98

ALSO AVAILABLE:

Sleeping With The Past
Piano · Vocal · Guitar
£6.95

The Very Best Of
Piano · Vocal · Guitar
£10.95

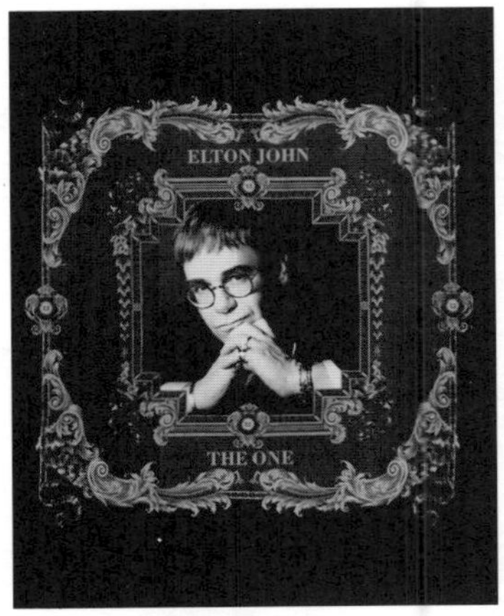

The One
Piano · Vocal · Guitar
£6.95

Duets
Piano · Vocal · Guitar
£6.95

Made In England
Piano · Vocal · Guitar
£6.95

Love Songs
Piano · Vocal · Guitar
£9.95

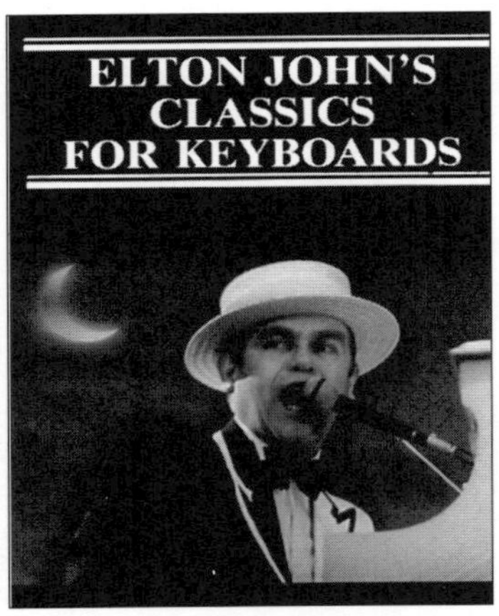

Classics For Keyboards
Solo Piano/Keyboard
£5.95

Classics For Keyboards 2
Solo Piano/Keyboard
£5.95

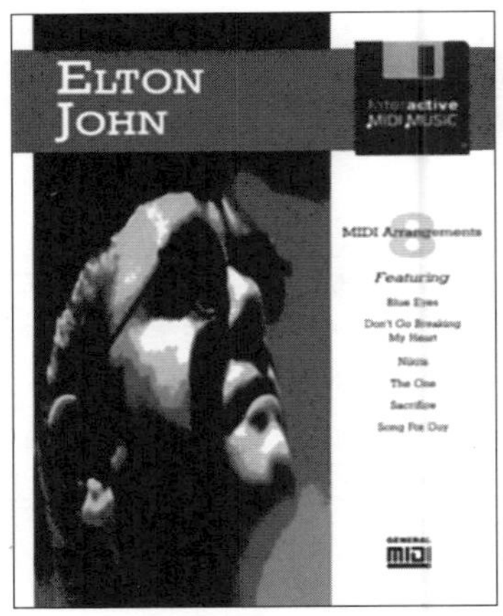

Interactive MIDI Music
General MIDI Disk · Songbook
£15.95

FROM ALL GOOD MUSIC STORES
If you have difficulty finding these products,
please contact Music Mail on: Freephone 0800 376 9100

IMP

International Music Publications Limited
Southend Road, Woodford Green, Essex IG8 8HN, England